Pebble® Plus
Bilingüe/Bilingual

Ciencia física/Physical Science

Todo sobre la temperatura/

All About Temperature

por/by Alison Auch

CAPSTONE PRESS
a capstone imprint

Pebble Plus is published by Capstone Press,
1710 Roe Crest Drive, North Mankato, Minnesota 56003.
www.capstonepub.com

Library of Congress Cataloging-in-Publication Data
Auch, Alison.
  [All about temperature. Spanish & English]
  Todo sobre la temperatura / por Alison Auch = All about temperature / by Alison Auch.
  p. cm.—(Pebble plus bilingüe. Ciencia física = Pebble plus bilingual. Physical science)
  Includes index.
  Summary: "Simple text and color photographs introduce temperature, including how thermometers work and the Celsius and Fahrenheit scales—in both English and Spanish"—Provided by publisher.
  ISBN 978-1-4296-6904-7 (library binding)
  1. Temperature—Juvenile literature. I. Title. II. Title: All about temperature. III. Series.
QC271.4.A82918 2012
536'.5—dc22   2011000639

Editorial Credits
Gillia Olson, editor; Strictly Spanish, translation services; Veronica Correia, designer; Danielle Ceminsky, bilingual book designer; Eric Gohl, media researcher; Laura Manthe, production specialist

Photo Credits
Alamy/Eric Chahi, 19
Capstone Studio/Karon Dubke, 7, 9 (all), 20–21 (all)
iStockphoto/Maria Pavlova, 1
Shutterstock/Armin Rose, 17; Junial Enterprises, cover; Karla Caspari, 11; Mandy Godbehear, 5; Rob Marmion, 15; Roman Sigaev, 13

Note to Parents and Teachers

The Ciencia física/Physical Science series supports national standards related to physical science. This book describes and illustrates temperature in both English and Spanish. The images support early readers in understanding the text. The repetition of words and phrases helps early readers learn new words. This book also introduces early readers to subject-specific vocabulary words, which are defined in the Glossary section. Early readers may need assistance to read some words and to use the Table of Contents, Glossary, Internet Sites, and Index sections of the book.

Printed in the United States of America in North Mankato, Minnesota.
122011
006506R

Table of Contents

Tabla de contenidos

What Is Temperature?

Have you ever been outside on a hot summer day? If so, you know about temperature. Temperature tells us how cold or hot something is.

¿Qué es la temperatura?

¿Has estado afuera en un día caluroso de verano? Si es así, tú sabes acerca de la temperatura. La temperatura nos dice qué caliente o frío algo está.

How a Thermometer Works

We use a thermometer to measure temperature. A thermometer's numbers and lines stand for degrees. The symbol ° also stands for degrees.

Cómo funciona un termómetro

Nosotros usamos un termómetro para medir la temperatura. Los números y las líneas en un termómetro representan grados. El símbolo ° también representa grados.

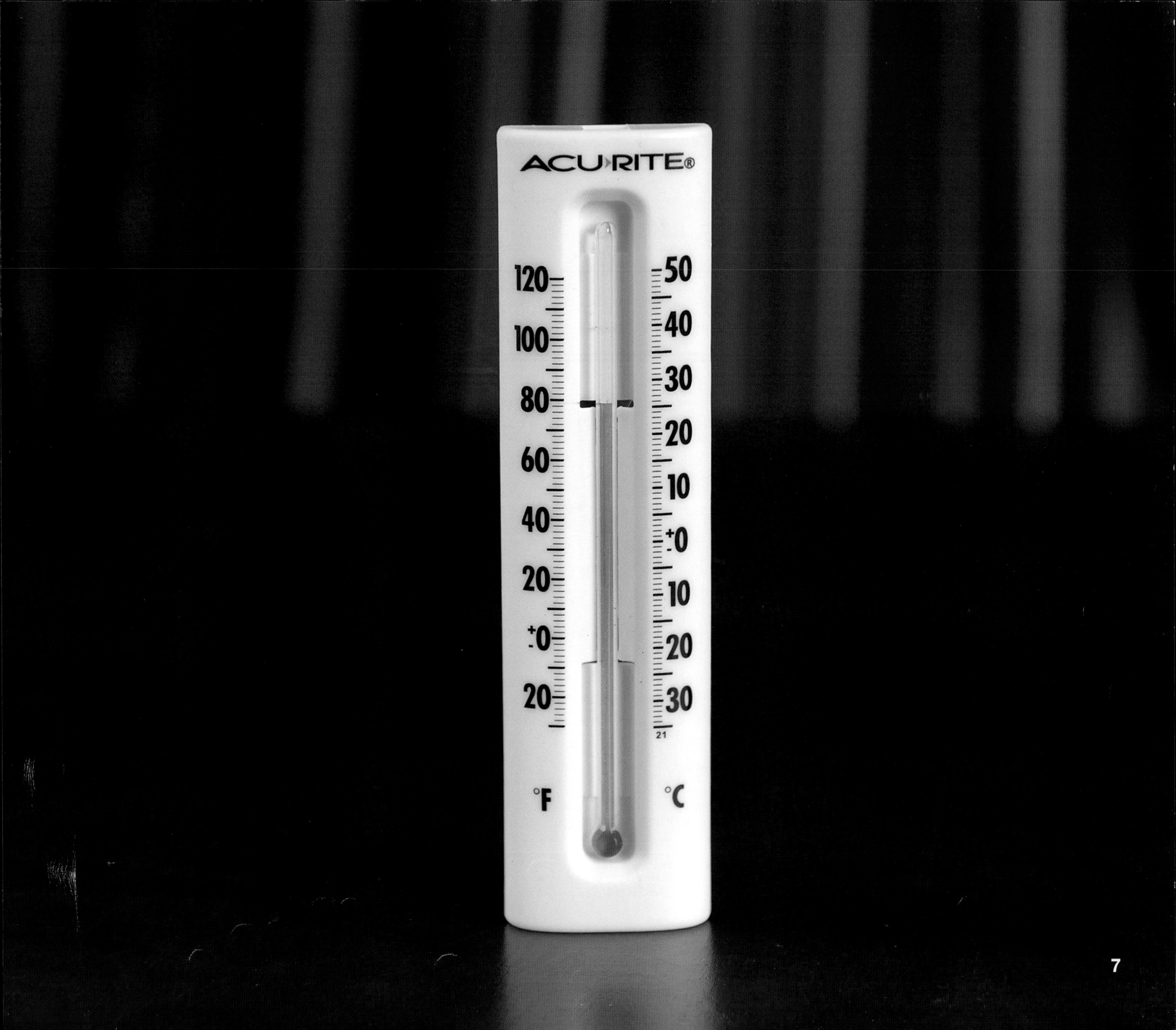
ACU-RITE®
120
100
80
60
40
20
±0
20
50
40
30
20
10
±0
10
20
30
°F
°C

In the thermometer is a liquid.
As the liquid warms, it expands
and moves higher up the tube.
As the liquid cools, it shrinks
and drops lower.

Dentro del termómetro hay un
líquido. Cuando el líquido se
calienta, se expande y se eleva
dentro del tubo. Cuando el líquido
se enfría, se achica y baja.

Celsius and Fahrenheit

Celsius and Fahrenheit are two ways to measure temperature. In the Celsius (C) scale, water freezes at 0°. Water boils at 100°.

Celsius y Fahrenheit

Celsius y Fahrenheit son dos maneras de medir la temperatura. En la escala de Celsius (C), el agua se congela a 0°. El agua hierve a 100°.

In the Fahrenheit (F) scale, water freezes at 32°. Water boils at 212°. To compare scales, water freezes at 32°F and 0°C.

En la escala de Fahrenheit (F), el agua se congela a 32°. El agua hierve a 212°. Para comparar las escalas, el agua se congela a 32°F y 0°C.

Temperature Facts

Temperature helps us measure important things. Most people have a body temperature of 98.6°F (37°C). A higher temperature can mean illness.

Datos de temperatura

La temperatura nos ayuda a medir cosas importantes. La mayoría de la gente tiene una temperatura corporal de 98.6°F (37°C). Una temperatura más alta puede significar una enfermedad.

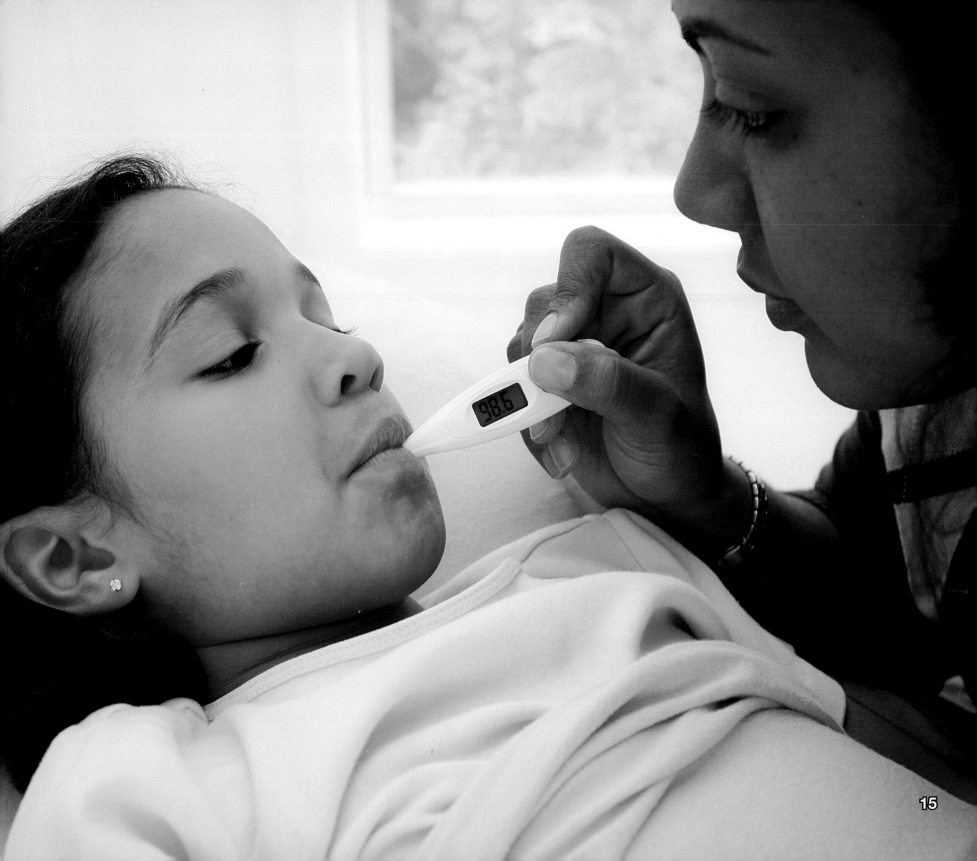

Some places are too cold
for people to survive outside.
In Antarctica the temperature
was once measured at 128°F
below zero (-90°C).

Algunos lugares son muy
fríos para que la gente pueda
sobrevivir afuera. En la Antártica,
la temperatura se midió una vez
a 128°F bajo cero (-90°C).

Some places get very hot. In 1922, the Sahara Desert reached 136°F (58°C). It was the hottest air temperature ever measured.

Algunos lugares son muy cálidos. En 1922, en el Desierto del Sahara la temperatura llegó a 136°F (58°C). Fue la temperatura de aire más caliente que se haya medido.

Make a Thermometer/Construye un termómetro

What You Need/Necesitas

- 12- or 16-ounce (355- or 473-mL) plastic bottle/ 1 botella plástica de 12 o 16 oz (355 o 473ml)
- food coloring/colorante de alimentos
- water/agua
- clear plastic straw/sorbete de plástico transparente
- modeling clay/arcilla moldeable

1

Put five drops of food coloring in the bottle.

Coloca cinco gotas de colorante de alimentos en la botella.

2

Fill the bottle 1/3 full with cool tap water.

Llena la botella a 1/3 con agua fría del grifo.

Hold the straw in the bottle so it's in the water but not touching the bottom. The top of the straw should stick out of the bottle. Mold clay around the straw to seal the top of the bottle.

Sostén el sorbete en la botella para que quede en el agua pero sin que toque el fondo. La parte superior del sorbete debe sobresalir de la botella. Moldea la arcilla alrededor del sorbete para sellar el extremo de la botella.

3

Hold the bottle in your hands for a few minutes. The heat in your hands will warm the liquid in the bottle.

Sostén la botella en tus manos por unos minutos. El calor de tus manos calentará el líquido en la botella.

4

Watch the liquid in the straw. The liquid goes up! The liquid in thermometers works in a similar way.

Observa el líquido en el sorbete. ¡El líquido está subiendo! El líquido en los termómetros funciona de manera similar.

5

Glossary

boil—to heat water or another liquid until it bubbles

degree—a unit for measuring temperature

expand—to get larger

freeze—to become solid at a low temperature

liquid—a wet substance that takes the shape of its container

measure—to find out the size or amount of something

shrink—to get smaller

Internet Sites

FactHound offers a safe, fun way to find Internet sites related to this book. All of the sites on FactHound have been researched by our staff.

Here's all you do:

Visit *www.facthound.com*

Type in this code: 9781429669047

Check out projects, games and lots more at
www.capstonekids.com

Glosario

achicar—disminuir de tamaño

congelar—convertirse en un sólido a baja temperatura

expandir—aumentar de tamaño

el grado—una unidad para medir temperatura

hervir—calentar agua u otro líquido hasta burbujear

el líquido—una sustancia mojada que toma el tamaño de su contenedor

medir—averiguar el tamaño o la cantidad de algo

Sitios de Internet

FactHound brinda una forma segura y divertida de encontrar sitios de Internet relacionados con este libro. Todos los sitios en FactHound han sido investigados por nuestro personal.

Esto es todo lo que tienes que hacer:

Visita *www.facthound.com*

Ingresa este código: 9781429669047

¡Algo súper divertido! Hay proyectos, juegos y mucho más en **www.capstonekids.com**

Index

Índice